# RAMADAN
## A Holy Month

By Malik Amin
Illustrated by Debby Rahmalia

🌹 A GOLDEN BOOK • NEW YORK

Text copyright © 2024 by Malik Amin
Cover and interior illustrations copyright © 2024 by Debby Rahmalia
All rights reserved. Published in the United States by Golden Books, an imprint of Random
House Children's Books, a division of Penguin Random House LLC, 1745 Broadway, New York,
NY 10019. Golden Books, A Golden Book, A Little Golden Book, the G colophon, and the
distinctive gold spine are registered trademarks of Penguin Random House LLC.
rhcbooks.com
Educators and librarians, for a variety of teaching tools, visit us at RHTeachersLibrarians.com
Library of Congress Control Number: 2023930086
ISBN 978-0-593-64944-2 (trade) — ISBN 978-0-593-64945-9 (ebook)
Printed in the United States of America
10 9 8 7 6 5 4 3 2

Tonight, we search the starry sky. We catch a glimpse of the crescent moon and begin holy Ramadan.

During Ramadan, Muslims eat and drink only when it is dark. We have a big meal very early—before the sun even rises—and we don't eat again until after the sun sets. This is called fasting. But why do we do it?

Because it is written in the holy book called
the Qur'an.

All Muslims follow the words of the Qur'an. It is read
around the world in many different languages.

The Qur'an tells us how to be a Muslim. For example, it says to care for people who need help, to pray five times a day—facing the holy city of Mecca—and to fast during the month of Ramadan.

But fasting isn't for everybody. Children and people who are sick are among those who do not fast.

Those who do fast start the day before dawn with a meal called suhoor. What we eat and drink before sunrise has to last us all day!

Eggs, oatmeal, potatoes, bread, rice, and nuts are good choices for suhoor. These foods give us energy. Some people eat fish or chicken, but nothing fried or too salty because that would make us thirsty during the fasting hours of the day.

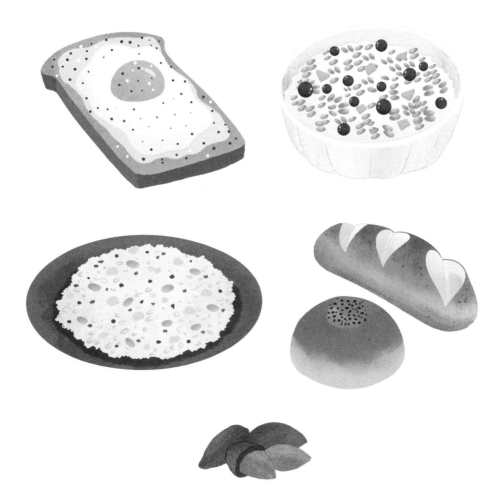

Fruits and vegetables like celery, cucumbers, lettuce, oranges, peaches, spinach, strawberries, tomatoes, and watermelon are full of water. Eating them helps us not drink until after sunset.

Ramadan isn't only about fasting. It's also about becoming a better person by being kind and helpful.

We raise money and give to those in need.
We spend extra time praying and reading the Qur'an.

We say, "Ramadan Mubarak!" to each other, which means "Happy Ramadan!"

And we prepare the food for our evening meal called iftar.

Muslims live all over the world and cook different, delicious meals. Some people start iftar with lighter food and a beverage, like a date with a glass of water or a sweet drink made with mixed fruits and syrup.

Others serve creamy curries, fresh soups, and rich stews. Fragrant rice dishes paired with grilled meat or kofta are popular. Crispy, golden pakoras filled with vegetables are a favorite in many families.

One thing is for sure: there's plenty of food for everyone as we sit together before another day of fasting.

Ramadan goes on for a whole month. It ends how it starts, with a crescent moon in the sky. This marks the beginning of a new month, Shawwal, and the celebration of Eid al-Fitr.

In Arabic, "eid" means "festival," and "al-Fitr" means "breaking of the fast." We call it Eid for short and we say: "Eid Mubarak!"

We dress in beautiful, new clothes and go to mosque and pray together.

After prayer, the celebrations begin! We visit our family and friends. We tell stories. We give each other presents. We decorate our homes with string lights and garlands. Some people use henna to decorate their hands, too!

And we cook our favorite foods.

Like suhoor and iftar, what we eat at the end of Ramadan is different from place to place, and family to family, all around the world. But no matter how we celebrate, Ramadan is one of the holiest times of the year for Muslims everywhere!

# A Glossary of Words and Phrases

**Eid al-Fitr** (eed al-FI-ter): the fast-breaking festival and first day of Shawwal

**Eid Mubarak!** (eed moo-BAH-rahk): Happy Festival!

**Henna** (HEH-nuh): a plant-based dye

**Iftar** (IF-taar): the fast-breaking meal after sunset during Ramadan

**Kofta** (KAAF-tuh): spiced meatballs

**Pakoras** (puh-KAW-ruhz): fritters

**Qur'an** (kr-AAN): the holy book of Muslims

**Ramadan** (RAA-muh-daan): the ninth month of the Islamic calendar

**Ramadan Mubarak!** (RAA-muh-daan moo-BAH-rahk): Happy Ramadan!

**Shawwal** (shuh-WAHL): the tenth month of the Islamic calendar

**Suhoor** (suh-HOR): the first meal of the day during Ramadan before sunrise